SHONEN JUMP'S

# Yu-Gi-Oh!™

THE ULTIMATE COLLECTOR'S CLUB

# YAMI MARIK

## the official character & monster guide

### by Arthur "Sam" Murakami

SCHOLASTIC INC

New York  Toronto  London  Auckland  Sydney
Mexico City  New Delhi  Hong Kong  Buenos Aires

Cover/Interior design: Julia Sarno

© 1996 Kazuki Takahashi

All rights reserved. Published by Scholastic Inc.

SCHOLASTIC and associated logos are trademarks
and/or registered trademarks of Scholastic Inc.

ISBN: 0-439-87920-5

12 11 10 9 8 7 6 5 4                    7 8 9 10 11/0

Printed in the U.S.A.

First printing, June 2006

# MARIK

# THE TOMBKEEPER LEGACY

The cold and nefarious Marik Ishtar was relentless in his quest to steal Yugi's Millennium Puzzle and destroy the Pharaoh. However, don't think that Marik was always evil. Believe it or not he was a curious and extremely affectionate child when he was young. How did Marik change from a kind soul to one of Yugi's greatest foes?

Marik was born into a family of Egyptian tombkeepers—whose mission was to protect two Millennium Items and the memories of the Pharaoh. For thousands of years, the family of tombkeepers passed down this mission from generation to generation. Marik's father was a tombkeeper, which meant that Marik was next in line to carry on the legacy.

In order to become the next chief, Marik had to make many sacrifices. He had to follow strict rules and regulations, such as living underground and never seeing the light of day. Since Marik was forbidden to make contact with the outside world, he never knew what was beyond the walls of his home.

Marik hated being a tombkeeper. He didn't have any freedom and had to stay inside in the dark all day. His older sister, Ishizu, and Odion, tried to comfort Marik, but it was little use.

# FREEDOM FOR A DAY

**O**ne day, Marik couldn't stand being underground. He wanted to see what life was like on the outside under the bright sun. He didn't care if he was just outside for a short time. Although Odion and Ishizu were against the idea, they helped Marik escape. Marik finally saw what life was like in the outside world.

Marik enjoyed his time on the outside. He went to the local market and stared at people wearing fancy clothes. He saw TV for the first time. Life on the outside was new and exciting. It was short-lived, however. After an hour, Marik knew that he had to get home before his father found him missing.

When Marik tried to quietly enter his house, he discovered that his father had booby-trapped the entrance. Marik's father knew that he broke the rules and snuck out to the outside world.

# RISE OF YAMI MARIK

**M**arik's father was furious. He punished Odion for helping Marik escape.

Marik, driven mad with rage, unleashed the hatred bubbling within him for years. He turned into Yami Marik, his evil alter ego.

The dastardly Yami Marik used the power of the Millennium Rod to send his father into the Shadow Realm. Before things spun too far out of control, Odion stopped Yami Marik from overtaking Marik's soul. Odion sealed away Yami Marik, but the new and dangerous personality could not be permanently erased.

# HUNTING FOR RARES

**M**arik's hatred towards the Pharaoh grew. Marik believed that if the Pharaoh didn't exist, Marik would not have to become a tombkeeper. And if Marik wasn't a tombkeeper, he wouldn't have to live underground. He would be free. In addition, his evil alter ego, Yami Marik, wouldn't have sent his father to the Shadow Realm. Marik would have had a life—a lovely life.

Marik completely changed. He became the leader of the notorious Rare Hunters, a shadowy sect that would stop at nothing to acquire rare cards.

Marik soon stole two of the three legendary Egyptian Gods, the most powerful monsters in the game. All he needed was the last one, but Ishizu hid the card from him. Marik would not rest until he had the third card in his hands.

# BEGIN THE BATTLE CITY HUNT.

**W**hen Marik learned of Kaiba's Battle City Tournament, the Rare Hunters snuck into the competition. Kaiba's Battle City Tournament was the premier tournament in the world. Marik knew the world's greatest duelists—including Yugi—would enter and bring their rare cards with them.

Marik did anything to win, no matter how illegal it was. Before the tournament began, he sent out his Rare Hunters to challenge duelists for their rare cards. Joey was one of the victims, and the Rare Hunters took his Red-Eyes B. Dragon. Later, Marik gave the Egyptian God Card Slifer the Sky Dragon to his minion Strings. Marik had hoped to increase the odds of defeating Yugi. Marik even changed his name to Namu, and pretended to be Joey, Tristan, and Tea's friend so that he could infiltrate their group. Worst of all, Marik brainwashed Joey and Tea with the magic of his Millennium Rod.

In the end, Marik decided to take matters into his own hands and entered the Battle City Finals. In his Shadow Game against Mai, Marik erased the memories of her friends for every life point she lost, and then he sent her mind into the Shadow Realm.

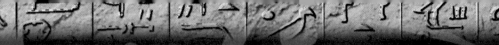

# RETURN OF YAMI MARIK

**D**uring the duel between Odion and Joey, Odion collapsed into unconsciousness. As such, Odion could no longer contain the seething evil hidden within Marik. Yami Marik returned, and he was more dangerous than ever before. With the Millennium Rod and the Egyptian God, The Winged Dragon of Ra, Yami Marik wrought havoc on everyone, sending Joey to the hospital and Bakura to the Shadow Realm.

With Yami Marik in control, regular Marik could only helplessly watch the chaos caused by his other personality. Marik finally realized the error of his ways. His misguided anger towards the Pharaoh not only broke his bond with Ishizu, but he also put Odion's life in peril. It wasn't Yugi's fault that the world was in danger—it was Marik's.

# REDEMPTION

In the last duel of the Battle City Finals, with the help of regular Marik, Yugi dueled against Yami Marik. Could Marik terminate Yami Marik for good?

Marik had one final task as a tombkeeper—he had to help the Pharaoh recover his lost memories. Not only did Marik give his Millennium Rod and The Winged Dragon of Ra to Yugi, but Marik also took off his shirt to reveal a tattoo on his back that was the key to unlocking the mysteries.

# ISHIZU

**PROFILE:**

name: Ishizu Ishtar
birthday: April 5
astrological sign: Aries
age: 20
favorite food: Om Ali
(Egyptian dish)
least favorite food: meat
family: marik Ishtar
(brother),
occupation: tombkeeper
chief (after marik's
disappearance)

# A SISTER'S LOVE

**E**ven after Marik formed the Rare Hunters and terrorized the world, there was one person who never wavered in her belief that there was still good within Marik—Marik's older sister Ishizu.

With her Millennium Necklace, Ishizu had the ability to see the future. She foresaw that if no one stopped Marik, he would bring the entire planet to the edge of chaos. Ishizu did her best to reason with Marik, but she failed, and Marik stole two of the three Egyptian Gods.

When Marik went into hiding, Ishizu could no longer find her brother. She had to find some way to bring Marik out into the open so that she could save him from the evil growing within his heart. She came up with a plan— a risky plan.

# ORIGIN OF BATTLE CITY

The only way Ishizu knew that Marik would come out of hiding was if the Rare Hunters could hunt for more than one powerful rare card at once. Therefore, she needed to gather a lot of strong duelists in one place, and what better place than a tournament. She knew of only one person who could make the tournament come true—Kaiba.

Kaiba was initially reluctant to help Ishizu, but Ishizu gave Kaiba the Egyptian God Card—Obelisk the Tormentor. Ishizu said that Marik would show up with his two Egyptian God Cards if Kaiba sponsored a tournament. Kaiba would also benefit from Ishizu's plan. He'd have a chance to win the God Cards and have the most powerful deck in the game. Kaiba agreed. The Battle City Tournament was on.

# CHANGE THE FUTURE

Though Ishizu asked for Yugi and Kaiba's help in stopping Marik, she knew that she would eventually have to save Marik on her own.

In order to duel Marik in the Battle City Finals, she had to defeat Kaiba first.

Ishizu wasn't worried because with the magic of her Millennium Necklace, she could see the future and know what Kaiba would do even before he did. She foresaw the perfect strategy to defeat Kaiba, so she was certain of victory. However, for the first time, her prediction failed. Kaiba had a trick up his sleeve. He changed the future. Ishizu could no longer see the future clearly, so she didn't know how the Battle City Finals would end up. Since anything could happen, she now needed faith that Yugi could save Marik.

ODION

Odion's parents abandoned their child when Odion was a baby. They left him next to a well. Fortunately, the Ishtars found Odion and decided to raise him. The childless Ishtars began to consider Odion as their heir to carry on the tombkeeper line. Life was great for Odion, but little did he know things were about to change.

## DUTY BOUND

When Marik was born, the Ishtars finally had a "real" son to carry on the tombkeeper legacy. Therefore, Odion lost his chance to become a formal member of the family by undertaking the tombkeeper's ceremony. Instead of being angry at Marik for this downturn, Odion loved Marik as his own brother.

Odion would do almost anything for Marik. When Marik wanted freedom and didn't want to be tombkeeper chief, Odion volunteered to take his place. Unfortunately, Marik's father unceremoniously dismissed Odion, saying Odion did not have the right to undergo the ceremony.

## BROTHERLY LOVE

When Odion helped Marik escape to see the outside world, Marik's father found out and punished Odion severely, which led to the rise of Yami Marik. Though Odion's love for Marik was able to suppress Yami Marik, Odion knew that the evil was never completely gone.

As Marik's anger towards the Pharaoh grew, it became harder and harder for Odion to contain Marik's hatred. At the Battle City Tournament, Odion served as Marik's right-hand man to help defeat Yugi and to make sure that the deep evil would not overcome Marik's heart.

During the Battle City Finals, under Marik's orders, Odion pretended to be Marik while the real Marik disguised his identity as the friendly Namu. Odion drew Yugi's attention away from the real Marik, allowing Marik to infiltrate Yugi's group.

In Odion's duel against Joey, Marik forced Odion to summon a fake version of The Winged Dragon of Ra, but Odion was punished for playing a phony card and was struck down by lightning. Odion fell unconscious and could no longer suppress Marik's evil, and Yami Marik emerged.

Although Odion was no longer awake, Odion and the good side of Marik still maintained their powerful bond. He could hear Marik calling out to him in his dreams, asking for help. Odion regained consciousness and crawled to the arena where Yami Marik and Yugi waged their final duel. Despite his weakness and fatigue, Odion managed to suppress some of Yami Marik's evil, allowing Yugi to defeat Yami Marik and rescue good Marik. Odion finally restored Marik to his kind self, and the family was reunited.

# RARE HUNTERS

**I**f you see suspicious duelists in dark cloaks and duel disks on their arms, watch out. They are the Rare Hunters. The Rare Hunters are Marik's notorious group of thieves who snatch rare cards from countless duelists to further their sinister schemes. With the power of the rare cards, the Rare Hunters were nearly unstoppable in any duel.

## THE FIRST RARE HUNTER

Joey encountered the first Rare Hunter when a corrupt game shop owner informed the Rare Hunter that Joey entered the Battle City Tournament. The Rare Hunter had lots of rare cards in his deck, including multiple copies of Exodia the Forbidden One. He obliterated Joey and took his Red-Eyes B. Dragon.

However, Yugi was able to get Red-Eyes B. Dragon back when he defeated the Rare Hunter and his Exodia the Forbidden One. How do you beat the unstoppable Exodia? Just don't let the Rare Hunter summon him.

# Arkana

The insane tuxedoed magician Arkana led Yugi to a circus tent of horrors. Arkana strapped Yugi's legs in chains to start the most dangerous duel ever—for every life point Yugi lost, a dark energy disc came closer and closer. A single touch from the spinning blade and Yugi was on a one-way trip to the Shadow Realm.

Arkana wanted to prove that he was the true magician, so he had a Dark Magician of his own. However, little did Arkana know that Yugi had a Dark Magician of his own, a female known as Dark Magician Girl.

Arkana seemed like the epitome of evil, but his life was one of tragedy. He used to be a great magician with a splendid life, especially since he had the love of his soulmate Catherine. They were going to get married, but when a dangerous magic trick—a trick he performed countless times perfectly—went awry, Arkana was left scarred and hideous.

Emotionally, Arkana couldn't bring himself to take the stage again. Catherine tried to heal his heart, but he was always angry because he lost everything. Before he knew it, Arkana was a broken man who drove Catherine away.

By the time Arkana figured out that he should have treated Catherine better, it was too late. She was gone. Arkana lost the love of his life.

Marik arrived and told Arkana that if he helped him defeat Yugi, he would use the magic of the Millennium Rod to win Catherine back. Arkana agreed and joined the Rare Hunters, but it was all a fake ploy. Marik never intended to help Arkana get Catherine back.

# strings

The mime duelist Strings never spoke, but his mighty Slifer the Sky Dragon did all the talking for him. Marik handed the Egyptian God to Strings so that he'd finish Yugi off once and for all, forcing Yugi to fight against his first Egyptian God ever. Marik even took over his mind so that Marik could force Strings to duel exactly as he wanted.

Fortunately, Yugi used his skills to exploit Slifer the Sky Dragon's weakness, making Strings run out of cards in his deck. With Battle City Tournament's ante rule, Yugi received Slifer the Sky Dragon. Marik wanted Yugi destroyed, but he unintentionally gave an Egyptian God to his hated foe.

# umbra & lumis

This masked duelist duo was ready to take down the top two duelists at the same time when they challenged Yugi and Kaiba to a terrifying duel on top of a skyscraper. The building's ceiling beneath their feet was made of glass, and if Yugi or Kaiba's life points ran down to zero, the glass would shatter. The losers would plunge hundreds of stories down to their doom into the Shadow Realm.

Yugi and Kaiba were better individual duelists than Umbra or Lumis, but they never worked together. Umbra and Lumis had the advantage because since they dueled as a tag team for a long time, they knew how to support each other perfectly. Meanwhile, Yugi and Kaiba's teamwork was ragged and unfocused because Kaiba only cared for himself.

In the end, Yugi and Kaiba were able to put their rivalry aside and work together as a cohesive team. Not only did they win, but they frustrated Umbra and Lumis so much that they were at each other's throats.

# MARIK'S MONSTERS

## THE WINGED DRAGON OF RA

| CARD STATS | |
|---|---|
| ATK: | NA |
| DEF: | NA |
| Level: | 10 |
| Attribute: | DIVINE |
| Type: | Divine-Beast |

**O**f the three Egyptian Gods, The Winged Dragon of Ra is the only one that can transform into different forms, each one with unique strengths and abilities.

## sphere form

Only duelists worthy of
its immense power can
control The Winged
Dragon of Ra. In
Mai's duel against
Marik during the
Battle City Finals,
Mai successfully
took The Winged
Dragon of Ra away
from Marik and into
her hand. However, when
she looked at the card, she was
unable to read the ancient Egyptian text written on it,
so The Winged Dragon of Ra stayed in its sphere form
and was completely useless.

# Dragon Form

When Marik chanted the ancient Egyptian text, The Winged Dragon of Ra slowly opened up, changing from its golden sphere form to a mighty dragon. Not only could The Winged Dragon of Ra emit a blazing blast from its mouth, but it gained power from its fellow monsters and even Marik.

# Egyptian God Phoenix Form

Like the mythological phoenix rising from its ashes, The Winged Dragon of Ra also returns from the graveyard in the form of a fiery phoenix. Engulfed in searing flames, it can burn all foes to ashes, proving that the Egyptian God Phoenix is nearly indestructible. With its divine heat, he charged and charred Joey into submission, sending him to the hospital.

# LAVA GOLEM

**M**arik's mighty Lava Golem is a unique monster. When Marik summons it to battle, he doesn't control it—his opponent does.

| CARD STATS | |
| --- | --- |
| ATK: | 3000 |
| DEF: | 2500 |
| Level: | 8 |
| Attribute: | FIRE |
| Type: | Fiend |

Marik gave Joey control of Lava Golem, and it turned out to be disastrous for Joey. Not only did the intense heat from Lava Golem's body drain Joey's stamina, but Lava Golem melted and dropped molten lava onto him, nearly burning Joey to a crisp. Joey couldn't escape from the lava even if he wanted to—he was locked inside the cage hanging from Lava Golem's neck. Therefore, beware: though Lava Golem is incredibly powerful, the drawbacks will make you sweat.

# LEGENDARY FIEND

**M**arik's Legendary Fiend is a hideous winged creature. Multiple heads and numerous claws purge out from different sections of its body, easily scaring the bravest of heroes into submission. Even worse, the longer Legendary Fiend stays out in battle, the more powerful it becomes.

In his duel against Joey, Marik used Legendary Fiend to destroy Little Winguard, but Joey managed to get rid of this menace by using the stunning power of Jinzo.

| CARD STATS | |
| --- | --- |
| ATK: | 1500 |
| DEF: | 1800 |
| Level: | 6 |
| Attribute: | DARK |
| Type: | Fiend |

There is no product development with Original Card Game.

# MAKYURA THE DESTRUCTOR

**Y**ou can't touch any part of Makyura the Destructor—its armor is sharp, the blades on its head are sharper, and the extremely long claws on its arms are the sharpest. Marik used Makyura the Destructor in his duel against Mai to slash his way past all her Amazons and claim victory.

| CARD STATS | |
|---|---|
| ATK: | 1600 |
| DEF: | 1200 |
| Level: | 4 |
| Attribute: | Dark |
| Type: | Warrior |

# DRILLAGO

**D**rillago's name says it all—its arms, head, legs, body and even its tail are made of drills. Spinning at incredibly high speed, these drills can bore holes into the toughest of hides.

Drillago was useful in various duels—Marik used Drillago to destroy Bakura's Puppet Master and Joey's Alligator's Sword.

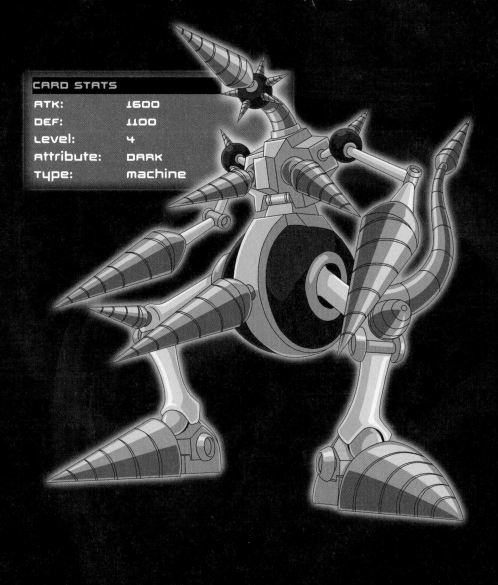

| CARD STATS | |
|---|---|
| ATK: | 1600 |
| DEF: | 1100 |
| Level: | 4 |
| Attribute: | DARK |
| Type: | machine |

# ODION'S MONSTERS

## CARD STATS

| | |
|---|---|
| ATK: | 2500 |
| DEF: | 2000 |
| Level: | 6 |
| Attribute: | EARTH |
| Type: | Fairy |

# MYSTICAL BEAST SERKET

**T**his huge scorpion-like monster guards the Temple of the Kings and the secrets contained within its altar. Don't be surprised if you only see its scorpion form for only a second – it evolves by snatching its foes in its pinchers and devouring them alive.

In Odion's duel against Joey, Mystical Beast Serket ate Jinzo, Insect Queen, and The Legendary Fisherman. Odion was about to terminate Joey by attacking with the advanced form of Mystical Beast Serket, but Marik stopped him and ordered Odion to use the fake The Winged Dragon of Ra to lay the final blow. Instead of victory, this maneuver led to disaster for both Odion and Marik because Odion lost the duel, fell unconscious, and Yami Marik took over Marik's body.

There is no product development with Original Card Game.

# EMBODIMENT OF APOPHIS

**E**mbodiment of Apophis is not just a monster or a trap. It's a new type known as a trap monster. Odion summoned this serpentine swordwielder in his duel against Joey, quickly confusing Joey because he had never seen a trap that was also a monster.

However, Joey eventually found the weakness in this Egyptian reptile. Though Embodiment of Apophis had the advantage of being both a monster and a trap, it also had the disadvantage of being a monster and a trap. When Joey destroyed its trap side, the monster was also destroyed.

## CARD STATS

| | |
|---|---|
| ATK: | 1600 |
| DEF: | 1800 |
| Level: | 4 |
| Attribute: | EARTH |
| Type: | Reptile |

# ARKANA'S MONSTERS
# ARKANA'S DARK MAGICIAN

**Y**ugi wasn't the only one to have a Dark Magician; the trickster duelist Arkana had one too. However, each Dark Magician reflected its owners' personalities – while Yugi's Dark Magician looked noble and confident, Arkana's Dark Magician was full of danger and malice.

Yugi and Arkana had their Dark Magicians battle to see who truly was the master of magicians. Arkana quickly gained the advantage by hitching Yugi's Dark Magician to a post. However, Yugi and his Dark Magician proved to have a stronger bond when Arkana was willing to sacrifice his Dark Magician carelessly for a chance at victory.

## CARD STATS

| | |
|---|---|
| ATK: | 2500 |
| DEF: | 2100 |
| Level: | 7 |
| Attribute: | DARK |
| Type: | Spellcaster |

There is no product development with Original Card Game.

# DOLL OF DEMISE

**T**his doll is not something you want to play with because it's neither cute nor cuddly. Besides, it wields an axe. Arkana combined Doll of Demise with Ectoplasmer to drain the monster's soul and strike Yugi directly.

| CARD STATS | |
|---|---|
| ATK: | 1600 |
| DEF: | 1700 |
| Level: | 4 |
| Attribute: | DARK |
| Type: | Fiend |

# UMBRA & LUMIS'S MONSTERS

# MASKED BEAST DES GARDIUS

| CARD STATS | |
|---|---|
| ATK: | 3300 |
| DEF: | 2500 |
| Level: | 8 |
| Attribute: | DARK |
| Type: | Fiend |

The masked duelists Umbra and Lumis used various spells, traps and monsters that involved masks, and the mightiest of their monsters was Masked Beast Des Gardius. Masks covered each of its three heads, and no one could even imagine what hideous visages they hid underneath.

Umbra and Lumis used this wretched monster against the tag team of Yugi and Kaiba, and Masked Beast Des Gardius shredded Blue-Eyes White Dragon with one swipe of its claw.

There is no product development with Original Card Game.

**M**arik and his Rare Hunters terrorized their opposition with their monsters.

## MARIK

| Monster | Attacks/Special Abilities |
|---|---|
| Drillago | Spiral Thrust |
| Makyura the Destructor | Three Claw Slash |
| Plasma Eel | Plasma Grip |
| The Winged Dragon of Ra | Blaze Cannon |

## RARE HUNTER

| Monster | Attacks/Special Abilities |
|---|---|
| Exodia the Forbidden One | Obliterate |

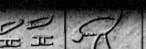

Check out the names of their devastating attacks.

# ARKANA

| Monster | Attacks/Special Abilities |
|---|---|
| Dark Magician | Dark Magic Attack |

# UMBRA & LUMIS

| Monster | Attacks/Special Abilities |
|---|---|
| Melchid the Four-Face Beast | Quadruple Smash Attack |

**M**arik and his minions are a curious lot. They are evil, they are dastardly. Don't believe what they say. Each will use their monsters to their full advantage.

| EP# | Episode Title | Monster | First Played By |
|-----|---------------|---------|-----------------|
| 55 | Stalked By the Rare Hunters | Hannibal Necromancer | Rare Hunter |
| | | Three-Headed Geed | Rare Hunter |
| 56 | Yugi vs. Rare Hunter - | Stone Statue of the Aztecs | Rare Hunter |
| | Part I - Battle City Begins | Gear Golem the Moving Fortress | Rare Hunter |
| 61 | The Master of Magicians- Part II | Doll of Demise | Arkana |
| 65 | Mime Control - Part I | Humanoid Slime | Strings |
| | | Worm Drake | Strings |
| | | Humanoid Worm Drake | Strings |
| | | Revival Jam | Strings |
| | | Slifer the Sky Dragon | Strings |
| 70 | Double Duel - Part I - Yugi and Kaiba vs. Lumis and Umbra | Shining Abyss | Umbra |
| 71 | Double Duel - Part II -Yugi and Kaiba vs. Lumis and Umbra | Grand Tiki Elder | Lumis |
| 72 | Double Duel - Part III - Yugi and Kaiba | Melchid the Four-Face Beast | Lumis |
| | | Rogue Doll | Lumis |
| | | Masked Beast of Des Gardius | Lumis |
| 86 | Awakening of Evil - Part I | Embodiment of Apophis | Odion |
| 87 | Awakening of Evil - Part II | Mystical Beast Serket | Odion |
| 91 | Mind Game - Part II - Mai vs. Marik | Makyura the Destructor | Marik |
| | | The Winged dragon of Ra (real) | Marik |

Check out and the first appearance of the monsters these and other duelists played.

| EP# | Episode Title | Monster | First Played By |
|---|---|---|---|
| 93 | A Duel With Destiny - Part I - Kaiba vs. Ishizu | Keldo | Ishizu |
| | | Mudora | Ishizu |
| | | Zorga | Ishizu |
| 94 | A Duel With Destiny - Part II - Kaiba vs. Ishizu | Kelbek | Ishizu |
| | | Agito | Ishizu |
| 96 | Showdown in the Shadows - Part I - Marik vs. Bakura | Drillago | Marik |
| 122 | Back to Battle City - Part I | Newdoria | Marik |
| 123 | Back to Battle City - Part II | Lord Poison | Marik |
| 124 | Back to Battle City - Part III | Dark Jeroid | Marik |
| 125 | The Darkness Returns - Part I | Gil Garth | Marik |
| | | Helpoemer | Marik |
| | | Plasma Eel | Marik |
| 126 | The Darkness Returns - Part II | Lava Golem | Marik |
| | | Legendary Fiend | Marik |
| 127 | The Darkness Returns - Part III | The Winged Dragon of Ra (Egyptian God Phoenix form) | Marik |
| 138 | The Final Face-Off - Part I | Juragedo | Marik |
| | | Vampiric Leech | Marik |
| 140 | The Final Face-Off - Part III | Bowganian | Marik |
| | | Egyptian God Slime | Marik |
| | | Metal Reflect Slime | Marik |
| 141 | The Final Face-Off - Part IV | Indestructable Egyptian God Slime | Marik |

# DID YOU KNOW...

...that Umbra means "dark" and Lumis means "light?" You can tell which duelist is which by looking at their masks. Umbra has a dark mask while Lumis has a bright one.

...that Odion became part of the Ishtar family before Marik? Odion was adopted by the Ishtars before Marik was born.

...that though Marik and Yami Bakura worked together to take down Yugi, they eventually battled each other in the end? Furthermore, Marik and Yami Bakura teamed up to duel Yami Marik.

...that when Marik and Ishizu were children, they met the mysterious Shadi? When Marik snuck out of his underground home and went to the market, Shadi was there.